Contents

The Art, Craft and Business of

Balloon Decorating

A Step-by-Step Training Manual

By

Ruth Younger

Revised and Updated

No part of this book may be reproduced or used in whole or in any part any manner or by any means whether graphic, electronic, optical or mechanical, including without limitation, photocopying or otherwise, without the prior written consent of the author in each instance.

www.balloonmanual.com
info@balloonmanual.com

ACKNOWLEDGEMENTS

This book would not have been possible without the love, help and support of my family. Thank you to Jim, my husband, for his patience and all the long hours of computer arrangements. To Kelly, for sharing his humor, time and consistency in proof reading to the final copy. To Steve, for his encouragement and assistance in finalizing the "book" and to Terre, for her constant support and diligence working with all the photographs.

To all my students over the years who helped make my seminars enjoyable. I wish you all the success you deserve in your new business.

INTRODUCTION

Who would have thought a helium tank and a bag of red balloons could change a person's life? Well, it did.

Searching for a small business as a second income, I happened to meet a woman at a night class. She was late because she had been decorating with balloons for a large corporation. I was intrigued with the idea of balloons and decorating. Creating themes for events and party planning was a business I had always dreamed about.

After a short conversation, I asked her if I could hire her to show me everything she could about balloon decorating. I spent the following Saturday in her garage learning how to handle helium tanks and blow up balloons. I bought one of her older small tanks for $50.00 and went home to practice.

When I told my husband I was going to start a balloon business, he envisioned my standing on street corners in a clown suit selling five foot long balloons. He wondered why I didn't just get a second job at Disneyland.

When he started to see my business "expand" it wasn't too long before he offered to become a partner. I let him be the partner who carried the heavy tanks, lifted the heavy supply boxes, and climb the ladder when we placed our designs. He has his own full time business, so I could not possibly make him a full partner. He had to be content to watch my bank account grow and work his way up in my company!

The balloon business is a great business for two people. If you have a supportive spouse, or young adults in high school who can help you, commission them. My son was very efficient. I could send him on a job and knew it would be excellent. I have employed many high school students during my years of business and always could depend on them.

1

A friend of my son, trained with me and went on to open his own balloon business. Pay the young people well. They will always be eager to help.

My first job consisted of building a 30-foot arch for a friend's wedding as a gift. As a result of this gift I received several calls and booked another wedding for three months later. The hotel asked for cards to give to their clients for decorating the ballrooms. Before long, I was booking two or three weddings every Saturday.

My First Free Event

Eventually, I decorated a warehouse for the Rose Parade! General Motors used the warehouse to build their float, then after it was moved out we constructed several 100 foot arches. We inflated football shaped balloons as centerpieces for the tables. Star shaped foil balloons covered all the tall pillars. This paid over $4,500 for only 10 hours work. I hired a crew of four students and we were all very proud of the finished picture, so was the Western Division CEO of General Motors.

Rose Bowl, General Motors

Hopefully you will find this book a valuable training manual to read and as a reference when you have questions. Remember I didn't have a book when I started so you are sharing in my successes and mistakes.

I will not only show you how to do balloon decorating but share my humorous stories, pictures and simple step-by-step methods. What other business do you know of that can be so profitable with just three little words, blow, tie, and float.

CHAPTER ONE

WELCOME TO THE WORLD OF BALLOON DECORATING!

Once you learn the basic steps to balloon decorating, your business will "expand" beyond your wildest dreams. Balloon decorating can be linked to many small businesses.

When I started out as a wedding coordinator over six years ago, I found myself hired by young couples to coordinate their weddings and arranging for the reception decorations. The two businesses complement each other.

Balloons are the up and coming decorations for weddings. They add color, fill in air space, and make a room festive. Balloons are less expensive than flowers and have a look of excitement. All of us remember having balloons as a child. It brings out the "little child" in us when we see them.

My book will be somewhat geared toward wedding decorating, but I will touch on other avenues for you to pursue with your balloon business.

Contact public and private high schools within twenty-five miles of your business and let them know you decorate for proms, Christmas Balls, homecoming games, outdoor and indoor dances, and for any other occasion. Your expense will be less for schools because the students always have a committee of volunteers to help decorate. You do not have to pay a crew to do the work. In this way you can give the school a break in price.

The more generous you are initially; usually the more generous they are for their next event.

Most high schools have a budget allowed for decorations for any of their large functions. Work on designs that will fit their budget and still give you a great profit. After you know their budget, meet with the committee to explain your ideas.

Locate your local colleges and contact the School Activities Department. Ask for their name and send your brochures and cards to be put up on the Student Affairs bulletin board. Find out the names of the sorority and fraternity presidents. Explain to them that you can do their insignias in balloons and lights in any size they require.

A local university fraternity asked me to create their insignia in balloons with lights for their formal at a hotel. I received several bookings just by leaving my cards with the director of the catering department.

Check with your local hospitals and leave your cards with the public relations representative. Many hospitals have balloon releases celebrating a special occasion, opening a new wing, fund raisers, or employee Christmas parties.

Hotels are happy to give out your information to business leaders who are putting together a large promotional banquet or planning a nationwide corporate meeting. A local hospital contracted me to decorate for an annual auction and fundraiser. They had a budget of $1,800. I had previously decorated for their employee banquet parties so they knew my work.

I spelled out the initials of the hospital in four-foot letters and suspended them with monofilament line in the hotel lobby. We decorated 50 tables with miniature Christmas trees. At least 50 bouquets of balloons were placed around the ballroom. The finished look was elegant. The director received all the applause and I received the $1,800.

Hospital Fund Raiser

Many of the program directors are happy to hand you the responsibility of decorating. You do the creating, the work, and they can take the credit for the wonderful finished look. You get to take the profit to the bank.

7

Automobile dealerships use balloons to call attention to their site. Ask for the manager and show them your balloon designs. The balloons have to be replaced daily if they are helium, and every few days if air is used. Be sure you include your time and labor for these jobs.

Grand openings for fast food companies are especially profitable; I decorated for a grand opening that lasted for a week. Part of the grand opening promotion included a new automobile that was being given away. It was in front of the building. I built helium filled single arches all around it every day for two weeks.

Grand Opening

Taco Bell booked us to put up an arch made of air inside their building. They kept it up for three weeks. Watch for construction of new buildings and call for the public relations department headquarters.

Hotels, restaurants, and reception halls have guests and prospective banquet room renters that ask for decorations for celebrating weddings, anniversaries, birthdays, graduations and employee parties. Again, get to them first. Don't wait around for business.

"SO I FORGOT A COUPLE OF DETAILS"

One summer I had to fly to Washington for a funeral. I booked a class reunion with a group of people from Kentucky. The hotel was in Long Beach and this group reunited every 10 years at the same place.

Plans were made over the telephone months ahead. All the details were on paper, the address of the hotel, colors to be used, and what balloon sculptures were to be designed. I left all the information for my husband and son. Confident that all would go well, I went on my trip.

My husband and son and another employee set out in plenty of time to complete the booking. They followed the set-up I had left, making several quad arches, decorating tables and bouquets.

As they were working, a group of people came into the room and started to set up for balloon decorating. This group looked at my group and my group looked back. We had purple and gold balloons already up and they were starting to inflate black and silver. Panic set in. My crew rushed out to the desk, paged the director of catering, and to their surprise were told they were decorating the WRONG class reunion.

Now the scene changes showing my crew twisting around a twenty-five foot quad arch to fit on an escalator to go up two floors.

As you will learn, the helium arch automatically flies up and trying to hold it down is not easy. Everything had to be moved via escalator. The reunion was on the third floor.

When I arrived home two days later, they threatened to resign forever.

ALWAYS VERIFY THE LOCATION OF THE EVENT!

CHAPTER TWO

STARTING YOUR NEW BUSINESS

MOTIVATION:

There are no secrets for a successful business but there are proven rules and procedures to follow. You always need knowledge and planning. Some eager people will jump into any business without understanding all the complex problems that are before them.

First of all to start your own business, you must believe in yourself. You can choose either faith or fear. One of these two emotions will dominate your life and determine if you fail or succeed.

When you set out to start your own business and things don't go right, never quit; simply adjust. Revise your time, scale down the size of your plans, and rearrange all your resources. You need to know this early on. When you start out to form your business, take each day in stride and stay motivated.

PERMITS AND LICENSES:

Starting your new business can be both exciting and overwhelming. The exciting part is putting your ideas into action. The overwhelming part is with the legal requirements you must meet in order to get your business started. The permits you need will depend on the type of business you plan to operate.

You may use your name or a fictitious name. You can just name it Balloons by Mary Jones if you prefer not to file for a DBA or "Doing Business As."

If you choose to conduct business under a name other than your legal name, you need to file a Fictitious Business Name Statement with the County Clerk's Office. This can be filed within 40 days of the first day of business: however, it is recommended that you file before opening your business to avoid confusion. Check www.Nolo.com for information to make sure no one else is doing business under the name you have chosen. After a Fictitious Business name has been filed, you will receive a certified copy of the application. The bank you choose for your business' financial transactions will request a copy of this certified form to open your account.

Within 30 days after filing a Fictitious Business Name Statement, you need to publish the statement in the newspaper of general circulation in the County. The statement must be published once a week for four weeks. Depending on the newspapers policy, either you or the newspaper will need to send proof of publication to the County Clerk. These newspaper offices will also file the County paperwork for a fictitious name, if you know that no one else is doing business under the name you have chosen.

If you don't want to do the footwork, you can use the internet www.filedba.com and it can all be done for you.

Your business name will be with you a long time. You need to keep the name descriptive, appropriate, and memorable. Using your own name is fine. Your personal identity is already in place and your business name can be a continuation of your recognition. Ten characters are about as long as you want to make it so it will fit on cards, letterheads, and invoices.

As you think about using your name, try not to get carried away with making your mark in history or handing the business down to your children. If it is appropriate, if it fits, if you like it, use it!

A Sellers Permit is required when purchasing wholesale products for resale. Because every state is different, you must contact your State Franchise Tax Board for instructions on how to get this particular permit.

This permit allows the Board of Equalization to keep track of your taxable sales in order to collect the sales tax you owe.

You will be issued a Sales and Use Tax Permit Number when you apply for a permit. In some states there isn't any fee for a Seller's Permit. A Driver's License is required as proof of identification.

Make a copy of your wholesale certificate and carry it with you. File the original in your new file cabinet. At the close of each quarter you will be mailed a form to fill out and return. You must file even if you did not have sales for that quarter. Simply mark it zero and return the form. If you owe money, send a check payable to the State Board of Equalization.

Once each year, every business is required to submit a Business Income Tax Statement to the Franchise Tax Board. For information regarding your filing, contact the State Franchise Tax Board or a private accountant.

For a City Business License contact the City Finance Department in your city. The city is interested in upholding the neighborhood. Keep the noise level to a minimum by not having heavy traffic coming to your home every day or UPS making frequent deliveries. Treat others like you want to be treated. Don't create a new freeway off ramp near your home for deliveries! Neither the city, nor your neighbors will appreciate it!

SECOND TIME AROUND

The high school football fans were filled with excitement, anticipating the homecoming game. I had been contracted to build a fifty foot balloon arch across the field with silver Mylar stars floating up from clusters of white balloon clouds.

Homecoming

Further down the stretch we would transform a wooden platform into a stage for the homecoming queen to be crowned.

I drew the plans to use miniature lights among the balloons and over the top of the platform. The Student Body moderator arrived three hours ahead of time to show us where to plug extension cords and how she wanted it set up. We had ample help from all the excited students.

We finished the fifty-foot arch and all the fluffy balloon clouds right on schedule and made our way through the heavy crowds with five people holding it. We set it up on the field within two minutes and bowed to the applause.

Homecoming platform

Next we ran with all our 18" silver Mylar stars and placed the clouds just right with the stars swaying in the wind. It was a masterpiece! The cheerleaders were in their places chanting for their team, the football players were ready to eat the opposing team alive and treat the audience to a great homecoming game.

Alive with excitement, suddenly the stadium lights went out! Complete darkness. Many minutes passed. Men with orange jackets were swarming around with flashlights checking outlets.

Forty-five minutes later an announcement was made "Due to electrical problems, the GAME WILL BE CANCELED, AND RESCHEDULED FOR NEXT FRIDAY EVENING AT THE SAME TIME."

There we stood; exhausted from the rush to finish on time, and now it was canceled. I spoke with the devastated moderator and explained that we would come back next week and repeat our work at no charge. She was so very grateful. She paid for the balloons and food, and for a DJ to play for the dance after the game.

One nice consolation was that she had one thousand cookies in the kitchen for the dance and knowing she couldn't save them, she shared many of them with us. So we went home on a sugar high and returned a week later. Our flexibility paid off tenfold as we were booked several months later to do their Junior/Senior prom.

KEEP UP YOUR SPIRITS AS WELL AS YOUR BALLOONS!

CHAPTER THREE

OFFICE EQUIPMENT AND SUPPLIES

Filing systems are one of the most important part of organization. If it is done correctly, it can save you from insanity. The IRS and your accountant will not look kindly on chaos, and their charges seem to have a direct correlation to your organizational skills.

When you start out, don't tie up your capital in office equipment. First, buy a file cabinet. It doesn't matter if it is two or four drawers. Buy hanging files or manila folders, and label them by subject. Some titles you might make for your folders are bank, vendors, clients, pending clients, accounts payable, suppliers, publications, and whatever other categories you need. Keep your customer lists on a computer with name, address, and phone number. Note the dates of contact and anything special to remember about your conversation over the phone to help you remember them personally.

Indulge in a desk and a chair. You won't feel like you are really in business until you have a desk. It doesn't have to be an expensive one. Think about your budget. Get a garage sale desk and spend your money on advertising. You will spend many hours in your chair. Make sure it is comfortable, and adjustable to support your lower back.

Your calculator should have a tape. It doesn't look too professional to whip out your cell phone with a tiny calculator in it. Clients are going to want to see figures.

Your telephone system is very important. Use your home phone as long as you can. You may want to add a line with a hold button or call waiting. If someone other than you will be answering the phone, be sure they are an adult and there is no background noise. It is better to have a separate number on your business card and have an answering machine so you won't miss any calls.

As I stated earlier it is important to have a separate office space. The dining room table will not work. You need to be able to leave your work and go back to it untouched by other hands.

When I interview clients, I make a pot of coffee and offer them a cup while we go over the event plans. I limit my time. I don't like to sit for three hours, share my expertise, and then have them say they will get back to me. Maybe they were just looking for ideas

"If you steal my purse you steal trash; if you steal my ideas you steal my gold."

I ask for a deposit for half of the job. The balance is due two weeks before the event. It is always difficult to receive the balance of your money after the party is over. If you are paid by check, this gives ample time for the check to clear the bank.

One office supply you will need is a telephone message pad. You will have a record of calls and can refer back if you need to. This may seem like a minor purchase. It is important to have the name and phone number, and what was discussed. You must always be consistent. If you quote $200 for a job over the phone, you don't want to give a $250 price at the interview because you forgot.

Invoice forms should have an original for the customer and carbons for your files. Have it state your business name and address, customers name and address, money deposited and any debts. If you know simple accounting, you can keep your own books. Buy a ledger book to keep track of which clients owe you money and in what amounts. Your invoice book and ledger book can be bought at a stationary store.

If you don't want to do your bookkeeping, there are many CPA's who will do it for you. Every three months you need to turn in your sales tax and form if you have a wholesale number.

Business cards are one of the most important supplies you will buy. They don't have to be fancy. All that is needed is your name, title or your business name, and phone number. On your business card, you may not want to put your own home address. There are private postal services. The cost is very reasonable and when you rent one, it gives you the right to use their street address. You can put a suite number or department number on it.

If you have the advantage of a fax machine, put the fax number on your card and have the look of a larger business. UPS or any delivery service can deliver to the private postal service and they will hold it for you.

Order a large quantity of business cards and leave them every place you go. Color cards are much more expensive but if you have the money, spend it. You can pick out logos from many of the books available. Perhaps a logo of a balloon to tell people what your service is.

If you have tried to start your own business in the past and it didn't work out, don't be a member of the "Moan and Groan Society." Now you are deciding to do something new. Your past is part of the learning process. Be patient with yourself.

Those of you who are already in a business and want to expand, good for you. Don't settle for a single business. Move ahead and open up new avenues. You are reading this book today, so you have already taken your first step.

NOTES

CHAPTER FOUR

SAFETY

"MAMA DON'T LET YOUR BABIES
GROW UP TO BE COWBOYS"

How many times have you seen young people talking like Alvin the Chipmunk because they inhaled some helium and it changed their voices? This was very funny to me until I found out helium could harm the lungs, or the person could suffocate.

I didn't have a balloon book to tell me about these dangers. I once caught my crew inhaling the helium while we were working. They would then sing Willie Nelson's *"Mama, Don't Let Your Babies Grow Up to be Cowboys"* to everyone's delight within hearing distance.

Helium is a very safe, non-flammable, odorless gas compressed in a metal cylinder. Because it is lighter than air, it is the gas used to inflate balloons so they will float.

Working with balloons is a business. You need to be informed of the facts regarding helium. Safety takes top priority in the balloon business today. All responsible balloon artists must be aware of the safety practices and safety equipment available.

1. DO NOT ALLOW ANYONE TO BREATHE HELIUM.

2. Always transport helium cylinders on a hand truck. (See Equipment Chapter)

3. Use cylinder wall brackets in the work place, these also can be mounted to the floor of a delivery van to prevent cylinders from rolling around during transport.

4. Shut off the tank before removing the regulator.

5. Do not place or store cylinders in direct sunlight.

6. Always use a weight on metallic and latex balloons even if it is a single balloon.

7. Metallic ribbon is prohibited on any helium-filled balloon.

8. Never release a metallic balloon as it can become entangled with electrical power lines.

ON-SITE SAFETY

Arrive early to the site, allowing plenty of time before the event. Banquet rooms are not always available on time from a previous party. This can cut down on your work time and you will end up decorating while the guests are arriving. If this happens, ask for a vacant room to do preliminary work. We once worked underneath a very warm stairwell to build our designs while waiting for a banquet room to vacate.

Always place your equipment in an area away from the workers of the site. Do not leave any boxes that a busy waitress could accidentally trip over. If you are using electrical cords, tape them to the floor to prevent accidents.

Leave one person with your equipment at all times. Take turns going for refreshments. Children are especially curious about balloons and could get hurt if a tank was pushed over.

When you are building an arch and need to stretch monofilament or balloon arch line across the room, make a cluster of 4 balloons and put them on the line every six feet. This will let people know to walk around.

ALWAYS USE THE SAFETY STAND FOR HELIUM TANKS.

CHAPTER FIVE

BALLOON EQUIPMENT & SUPPLIES

The helium cylinder is the main ingredient of the balloon business. The balloons would not fly without this odorless, colorless, and non-flammable gas. When a latex balloon is filled, depending on the size, it will last from 7 to 12 hours. A Mylar balloon can last up to three weeks if it is adequately sealed when inflated.

Helium tanks vary in weight and size. You will need to purchase a regulator with a gauge so you will always know how much helium you have in the cylinder. You will need to buy two tanks in order to use all of the helium in the first tank. If you need to use three-quarters of the tank on your first job you will only have one-quarter left for the next job, which is not enough. The suppliers will charge you for a complete fill even if some helium is left in your tank. If you purchase the large steel tank (290) and a transfer kit you will be able to fill the smaller lighter aluminum tank to take to the job site. This also saves extra trips to the supplier just for helium.

Once you have this purchase, you need only buy extra inflators to use on spare tanks when you have a lot of balloons to inflate. You can also purchase a multiple inflator which gives you three inflators on one tank. Visit several balloon distributor showrooms before you make your purchases.

When you are starting out, don't overbuy. Build up your business first then invest in more equipment. Your first job could buy a starter kit for around $600. Remember to get paid for the event two weeks in advance. I recommend an advance package for approximately $700. It includes a larger helium tank so you can book major events.

HELIUM CYLINDERS

The first major purchase for your new business should be a helium tank. When choosing a tank, keep in mind three factors: How tall am I? How strong am I? How many balloons do I need to inflate?

The largest steel tank on the opposite page is 290 cu. ft. of compressed helium gas will inflate 1000 nine-inch or 500 eleven inch balloons but weighs 144 lbs. and is 56" tall. This helium tank is ideal for keeping in a shop but is difficult to lift or fit into a trunk of an I automobile. It is also very difficult if not impossible to take up a flight of stairs.

The 137 cu. ft. helium tank is made of lightweight aluminum weighing only 50 lbs. and will inflate 500 nine-inch balloons. This is enough to do an average wedding.

The smaller the size of the helium tank the less economical it becomes to fill with gas. You could keep a large steel tank with a transfer hose at your business and fill a smaller portable tank from it.

The companies that fill your helium tank are required by law not to fill any tanks that do not have a safety cap. Always transport your tanks with the safety cap over the valve.

If you are considering buying a used tank, note the date stamped on the cylinder. After a certain time the tank must be water pressure tested and serviced. Ask your dealer.

Use the special tank dolly to move the tanks around. Never drag or pull the tank by the valve. Dragging can scar the base of the tank and weaken the metal. The valve is what holds the 2640 pounds of pressure inside. Don't store tanks in direct sunlight or in temperatures exceeding 130 degrees.

Never leave an unattended or unsecured tank in a hallway or where there is heavy foot traffic that could knock over the tank.

HELIUM CYLINDERS

Cu. Ft	PSI	No. of 9" balloons	No. of 11" balloons	No. of 18" foil
290	2640	1000	500	648
219	2215	700	400	484
137	1800	500	250	272
110	2216	400	200	222
88	2216	300	150	165
55	1800	200	100	125
41	1800	150	75	83
27	1800	100	50	60
14	1800	40	20	27

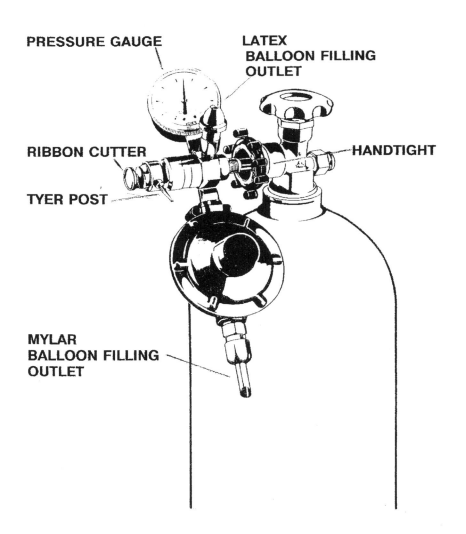

PRESSURE GAUGE

LATEX
BALLOON FILLING
OUTLET

RIBBON CUTTER

HANDTIGHT

TYER POST

MYLAR
BALLOON FILLING
OUTLET

AUTO-FILL MYLAR AND LATEX REGULATOR

AUTO-FILL MYLAR AND LATEX REGULATOR

BALLOON INFLATOR OPTIONS

Hand tight Cylinder Connection
Allows the user to connect the balloon inflator to the cylinder without the use of a wrench. The extended grip ring feature insures a leak-free connection.

Pressure Gauge
Provides an accurate cylinder pressure reading. This 2" diameter gauge enables the user to calculate how many balloons the cylinder will fill.

Auto-Fill Mylar Feature
Works on all size Mylar balloons and will shut off the flow of helium when the balloon is properly inflated. Mylar balloons are very sensitive to pressure.

Basic Push Valve is operated by placing the balloon over the tip of the valve and pushing down to release the helium.

Disc Tyer Post & Ribbon Cutter
Enables the user to tie the balloons with a small plastic disc. By holding the ribbon to the neck of the balloon and placing the balloon on the disc tyer post and sliding the disc over the neck of the balloon and ribbon in one motion, your balloon is sealed and tied to the ribbon.

The ribbon cutter is a small recessed blade the user slides the ribbon over.

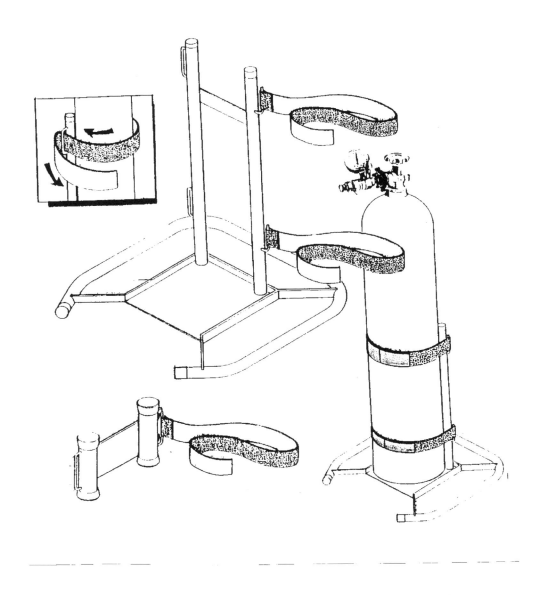

THE CYLINDER SAFETY STAND is designed to support all size cylinders. The cylinder safety stand is a must for worker safety in the shop and on the job. The flat cylinder base plate provides greater stability and ease in positioning cylinders. Two adjustable safety belts secure all size cylinders.

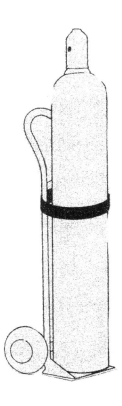

CYLINDER HAND TRUCK

Industrial strength reinforced steel
frame. Features large ball bearing
wheels and adjustable safety
chain.

4-WHEEL HAND TRUCK

This hand truck was designed for
the balloon industry to safely
support and transport helium
cylinders. It doubles as a
safety stand. It balances the
cylinder weight without operator
support.

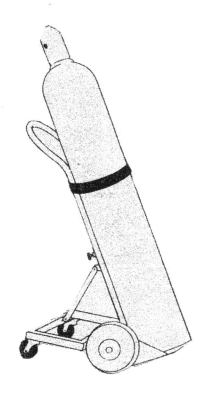

BALLOON HOLDERS

BALLOON HOLDER CYLINDER MOUNT

Adjustable belt
fits all size
cylinders.

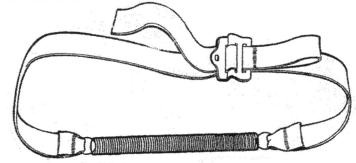

BALLOON HOLDER TABLE MOUNT

Thumbscrew tightens holder
to the table. The spring
holds the string or ribbon.

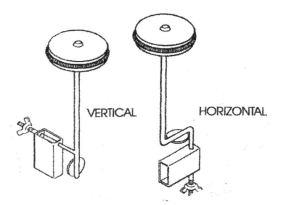

VERTICAL   HORIZONTAL

BALLOON HOLDER COUNTER TOP MOUNT

Drill hole in counter top
Insert rod and tighten.

ADDITIONAL EQUIPMENT

Conwin Carbonic Air-Pro countertop air inflator is ideal for fast inflation of your air-filled balloons. It inflates all sizes when you press down on the push valve outlet. The motor runs only when you are inflating balloons

Conwin Carbonic Air Force 4 air inflator features four outlets for simultaneous inflation. It maintains a fixed temperature and won't overheat. It is foot pedal controlled.

SUPPLIES

When you start your business one of the first steps is to organize a work area. Use one whole wall for your balloon supplies. Preferably, put up shelves over a worktable. Use boxes to keep your balloons sorted by size and color. Make a pegboard three feet long by two feet wide and mount it on the wall. Insert metal holders into the pegboard to hold your rolls of ribbon. Also, you can hang your scissors and tape on it.

BALLOON ARCH LINE

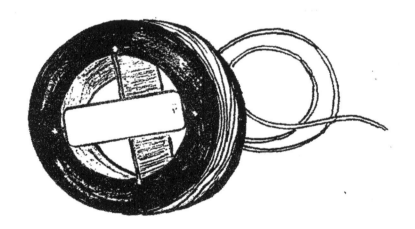

Dacron 50# Test Line grips the balloon more securely.
It will not stretch and is not affected by the temperature.

BALLOON TYING DISCS

Plastic tying discs are packaged 100 or a package of 1000. The tying disc eliminates having to tie the balloons with your hands.

BALLOON DISC TYER INSTRUCTIONS

1 PLACE DISC ON POST

2 HOLD RIBBON AND BALLOON TOGETHER WHILE STRETCHING BALLOON NECK. WRAP AROUND END OF TYING DISC.

3 SLIDE DISC OVER END OF POST AND DOWN 1-INCH ON BALLOON NECK.

4 REMOVE BALLOON FROM POST AND CUT RIBBON ON CUTTER.

WORK KIT

TYING DISCS	MASKING TAPE
CLIP-ON SCISSOR KEEPER	DBL STICK TAPE
BALLOON CADDY	RUBBER CEMENT
STAPLE GUN	DUCT TAPE
ADHESIVE GRIP-STRIPS	TRASH BAG
BALLOONS	RIBBONS
FLORAL PINS	TISSUE PAPER
STRAIGHT PINS	WEIGHTS
THUMB TACKS	SAND (funnel)
ARCH LINE (50# test)	ELECTRIC CORDS
MONOFILAMENT LINE (50# test)	LADDER
CLIP-ON ARCHLINE PACK	PHOTO ALBUM

BALLOONS

There are many brands of balloons to choose from, but I always recommend Qualatex. Pioneer Balloon Company is the manufacturer. They do not sell the balloons direct, but you can contact a distributor near you. The quality and color selection Qualatex offers can't be beat. Latex balloons are sold 100 per package.

STANDARD ASSORTMENT: red, blue, green, yellow, orange and pink. White can be added to the assortment if you request.

JEWEL-TONE ASSORTMENT: ruby red, emerald green, amethyst violet, citrine yellow, sapphire blue, quartz purple and diamond clear.

DEEP JEWEL-TONE COLORS: garnet wine, onyx black, and cocoa brown.

FASHION-TONE ASSORTMENT: wintergreen, spring lilac, hot rose, goldenrod, tropical tea, Georgia peach and ivory silk.

PEARL-TONE ASSORTMENT-pearl white, pearl mint green, pearl light blue, pearl azure, pearl mauve, pearl pink and pearl peach.

METALLIC COLORS: gold and silver.

GIANT 40" DISPLAY BALLOONS: pale blue, yellow, orange red, dark blue and green.

HEART ASSORTMENT: red, pink, white, ruby red, diamond clear, jewel tone assorted.

GEO DONUT & BLOSSOM: emerald green, sapphire blue, quartz purple, ruby red and citrine yellow.

260 ASSORTMENT: blue, orange, pink, white, ruby red, yellow, green, purple clear, and onyx black. These are sometimes used for animal balloon sculptures.

SUPER AGATE COLORS: primary (red, blue, yellow, green) fashion (light blue, pink, and white) black and white.

MYLAR (foil): plain and imprinted, all sizes, shapes, and occasions.

AIR WALKERS: character balloons

BALLOON FLYING TIME CHART

BALLOON SIZE - LATEX	AVERAGE FLYING TIME
9 inch	8 - 16 hours
11 inch	12 - 14 hours
14 inch	26 - 40 hours
16 inch	30 - 50 hours
40 inch	3 - 5 days
BALLOON SIZE - MYLAR	
18 inch	7 - 10 days
28 inch	10 - 15 days
36 inch	10 - 15 days

Actual flying time depends on temperature and conditions

INFLATING INSTRUCTIONS

LATEX BALLOONS:

1. Pinch latex balloon between thumb and forefinger and push down on brass inflating outlet to release helium. If using rubber valve, tilt forward to release helium.

2. When balloon is filled to desired size remove balloon inflating outlet.

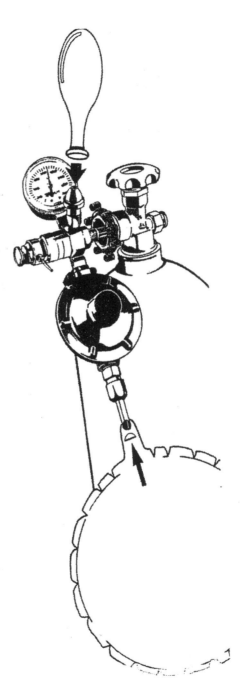

MYLAR BALLOONS:

1. Slide inflating outlet into neck of Mylar balloon.

2. Pinch the neck of the Mylar balloon between thumb and forefinger and push inflating valve upward to release helium.

3. When Mylar balloon is properly inflated the helium flow will shut off automatically.

37

ACCURATE INFLATION

Accurate inflation of latex balloons is the indication of a professional balloon business. It is recommended to use a template to size all your balloons. A template can be cut out of thin plywood or pressboard. Cut the circles in sizes of 5"-9"-11"-14"-16".

Place the balloon upside down over the desired size of the template. Deflate the balloon until it fits the opening. Now you will have all the balloons uniform in size and your sculptures will look professional.

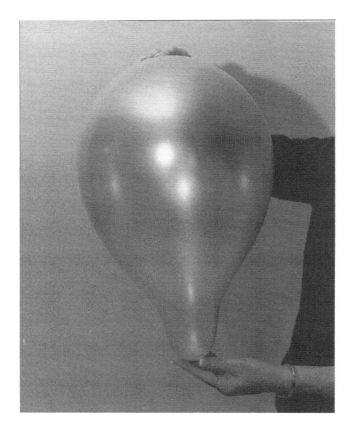

Over-inflated pear shaped balloon.

38

CHAPTER SIX

TERMS, MARKETING & PRICING

BASIC BALLOON TERMS

Air-filled: Balloons filled with air instead of helium.

Air Machine: An inflator operated by pushing down the inflation outlet.

Arch: A curved design having the form of an arch.

Arch Line: Dacron string of 50# test. Grips the balloon securely, will not stretch. Used for single and spiral quad arches.

Balloon Release: A container holding helium filled balloons to be released at a certain time. Large plastic balloon bags are generally used.

Basic Stand: This stand is made out PVC pipe (sprinkler) and is used for a variety of free-standing forms.

Caddies: A frame that fits around the cylinders, includes three bags to hold balloons, discs,   and ribbon. Creates an instant work station.

Cluster: Balloons tied together, Usually to form a sculpture.

Column: Quads of balloons placed on a PVC stand.

Discs: Round plastic clip with a hole in the middle that fits on the disc tyer post. The disc is used instead of hand-tying the latex balloon.

Foil: A term used for Mylar balloons.

Gauge: A device used to measure helium in a cylinder.

Helium: An odorless, colorless, non-flammable gas.

Latex: Synthetic rubber balloons.

Monofilament Fishing Line: a clear plastic line used to build balloon sculptures and arches.

Mylar: Another name for the metallic or foil balloon. Usually has messages written on them. Must be weighted by law.

Portfolio: A photo book of balloon displays used to market the service.

Post: Discs are placed on the tying post which is attached to the regulator. It is used to stretch the neck of the balloon and the ribbon over to secure the balloon.

PVC: Plastic sprinkler pipe used to design letters and numbers, and free-standing forms. It is used as a basic stand.

Regulator: Also known as an inflator. It is attached to the helium tank and is used to regulate the flow of gas.

Ribbon Dispenser: Free standing unit with a top feed to pull all the ribbon simultaneously.

Safety Stand: Flat cylinder base plate designed to support large cylinders.

Spiral Quad Arch: An arch made up of quads of balloons, with a swirl design throughout the arch.

Wall Bracket: Secures all size cylinders with an adjustable safety chain.

Weights: Used to anchor balloons. Sand, fishing weight, marbles.

Wire: Fence wire, (9 gauge) used to shape numbers, letters, and forms.

MARKETING

This book is geared toward a home-based business. This means you may not have foot traffic or a sign to advertise. The success of your business will depend on how you market your balloon designs.

When I first started out of my home, I set aside two days a week for promotion. Taking a different city each week, I placed my business cards in store fronts that related to weddings and event planning. The store owners were very happy to exchange cards when I informed them I was also a wedding coordinator. Networking with other vendors can be a great resource for you. If you are decorating for a wedding and the bride is looking for a photographer, she will certainly appreciate your recommendations, as will that vendor!

Map out all the hotels and large restaurants that have banquet rooms. Call the day before and make appointments with the Director of Catering to show them your portfolio. Ask to see the ballrooms and banquet area. Find out how you can be referred through the Catering office. Leave your cards and a brochure if you have one. Again, ask for their cards in exchange. If the Director of Catering refers your service, be sure and send them a thank you card.

Note where a bride and groom will shop to prepare for their wedding. Keep in mind the following:

Bakeries   Jewelers
Photographers   Florists

Party Rental Companies   Limousine Companies
Tuxedo Shops   Bridal Shops

Buy the plastic card holder (which cost under $3.00) and write the name of your business on the back of it. Many times if the cards run out, another vendor will just place their cards in.

Give the holder and your cards to the shops and ask if they will place it on top of the counter where it is visible. Keep a log of the places you have cards and go back periodically and refill their supply.

Anytime you see an "opening soon" sign, take the telephone number and offer your services for their grand opening. Sometimes the company will purchase a large amount of balloons to be given away to the children on their first day.

Beginning in October, contact large corporations and businesses regarding their company Christmas parties. Take a bouquet of balloons and several cards and leave them in the lobby with the receptionist. Find out who is in charge of decorations, and show them your possibilities. Take the responsibility out of their hands. They will be more than grateful that you called.

One large company calls every November and gives the date and time of their Christmas party at a nearby hotel. They give a budget of $1500 to $3000, leaving all the decorating up to me. Knowing this ahead, I purchase centerpieces during the summer at gift conventions and save a considerable amount of money. You have to earn the trust of your clients, which takes time, but cooperation and loyalty will ensure this.

Always, always, take pictures of balloon decorations that you design. Even if it is only a small job, TAKE A CAMERA. This is how to build a balloon portfolio. If you can afford to have a professional photographer take pictures of the designs, it will help you tremendously.

This portfolio helps show the client what you can do for them. Keep the album and cards in the trunk of your car. Many times, I have been running errands and realized I had met a potential customer.

Make up mini albums in three by five holders and leave these with the catering directors in large hotels.

PRICING

Pricing is strictly up to the individual. I will give you a guide that I use, but it depends on what is best for your small business. It is not wise to quote your price by single balloon. You are selling designs. Sometimes a customer might ask, "How many balloons will you put in the arch?" My answer is always the same: "I don't count the balloons; I will use whatever it takes to make your design perfect." You might get a customer who has nothing better to do with their time than to count each balloon used at their function! Always give the customer a price for each design and then a total price. Be sure you include travel time and any unusual circumstances. For example, hanging designs from a twenty foot ceiling might force you to rent a ladder.

Pricing must include the materials and labor. My rule of thumb is four times the total. If I spend $10 on supplies for a design, I will charge $40. When the job involves a delivery, there is an extra charge. I charge $10 for any delivery within a 20-mile radius.

I charge by the foot for spiral quad and single arches. Measure the distance for the spiral arch, plus the 10 feet for the height, take this total and multiply it by $8 per foot. For example, a 50 foot quad arch will sell for $400. A bouquet of balloons without a weight will average $2.00 a balloon.

You will need to determine your own price list. Each decorating job will involve different costs. When you are starting, you may want to keep your prices lower than the local storefront business. You are not paying the overhead, and can afford to work for a little less.

Another formula to use is to decide how many balloons you will need for the event. If this translates to approximately $2.00 per balloon then your designs were priced right.

CHAPTER SEVEN

WEIGHTS AND CENTERPIECES

"WEIGHT! IT'S GETTING AWAY"

I was decorating at a Country Club, waiting for the florist to show up with the flowers for the table centerpieces. I finished the balloon arches; the ceiling balloons, and was ready to finish the job as soon as the tables had three balloons attached to each flower arrangement. Soon the guests started arriving but the florist was not among them. Twenty minutes before the bride was due to arrive, I went to the catering director and asked her if she had thirty ashtrays. I taped the ends of the balloon ribbons under the ash trays. The florist failed to show.

Balloon centerpieces can be attached to a variety of weights. Rocks can be wrapped in tissue paper, and then placed inside a square of tulle or net. For a Quinceanera, I attached three balloons to a small candy dish filled with peach and white jellybeans. My appetite for jellybeans caused the centerpieces to shrink!

A plastic champagne glass filled with marbles and wrapped in net tulle with a large bow at the top is very economical.

Balloons can be secured to a potted plant by wrapping the end of a ribbon around a nail and pushing the nail into the dirt. If nails are not accessible, you can use wooden sticks. To add a finished look, attach a large bow of the same color theme.

Economical Weights
Below: Potted Plant Centerpiece

A bottle of non-alcoholic sparkling apple cider in iridescent cellophane wrap with a large bow is very affordable.

Wrap a box of Jell-O in silver paper with a ribbon and bow on it, to make it look like a gift. It is heavy enough to weight three balloons. Be sure when you are attaching balloons to the centerpiece to make the ribbons at least four feet high so people can visit across the table.

Sparkling Apple Cider Centerpiece

You can take a regular latex balloon, insert a funnel into the neck and pour sand into the balloon. Tie the balloon and wrap it with material matching the theme of the party. This is about the least expensive centerpiece you can make.

Fishing weights attached to monofilament line are used to weight balloons floating in a pool.

When you are creating bouquets for a delivery, you can tie the balloons to a coffee cup filled with Hershey kisses candy. If it is for a new baby, you could attach them to baby toys or a lovable teddy bear. Weights can change according to the theme of the occasion.

The universal weights for the balloon arches are bricks wrapped in foil. The single arch can be weighted with a half of a brick. You also can fill containers with sand and cover them with large bows. There are base plates available at the balloon supply stores for attaching arch line if it fits in your budget.

Centerpieces will vary in price. Clients may express the type of centerpiece they want, not realizing the cost involved. Be sure you know the exact cost of the items before you quote a price.

BOW MAKING
Courtesy of Stats Wholesale Floral Supply

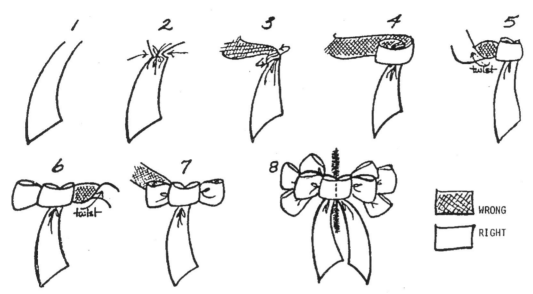

1. Measure off length of streamer-tail.

2. Pinch

3. Twist

4. Make a center loop.

5. Pinch and twist ribbon so right side is facing you.

6. Make a loop, pinch behind center loop, twist (right side up)

7. Loop, pinch and twist until you reach desired bow size.

8. Leaving enough length of ribbon to make the other half of streamer-tail, take a chenille stem, place it through the center of loop and around to the underside and twist.

NOTES

CHAPTER EIGHT

BOUQUETS AND BASKETS

Balloon bouquets are helium-inflated balloons that are attached to matching color ribbons. The traditional bouquet of multi-color balloons is characteristic of children's parties, birthdays, school functions and circuses.

Balloon bouquets can create a theme. If the bouquet is for Valentine's Day, it usually will consist of red and white hearts, round and Mylar balloons. This holiday calls for teddy bears and boxes of candy for weights. A "Happy Birthday" bouquet can be very personalized. Ask the client if the person receiving the bouquet likes a favorite perfume, a special hobby, or enjoys a certain gourmet food or coffee.

A popular design for a bouquet is to tier the balloons. Put two balloons higher on top, then three balloons a little lower by drawing down on the ribbons and doing the same to all the rest of the balloons. Make a handle with the ribbon by looping it and tying it. Attach the bouquet to a weight.

Remember to attach a card with the recipient's name. Ask the sender for the correct spelling of the name. Inquire if there will be a message on the card. Use a hand-held hole punch, make a hole in the upper left hand corner and thread a ribbon through it. Tie a knot on the underside to prevent the ribbon from slipping through. This method keeps the card intact with the bouquet.

Be sure you obtain the correct address, telephone number, directions, and the time of delivery. It is advisable to call ahead to insure the party will be there.

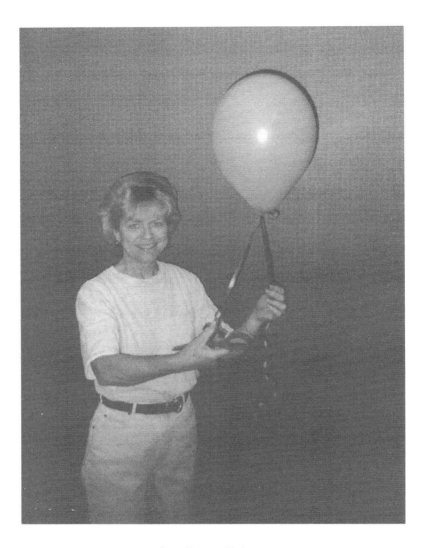

Curling ribbon

Cut the ribbons in six-foot lengths. Tie the ribbons between the neck with the clip and the inflated part of the balloon. Leave an extra foot of ribbon to curl with your scissors. Place the ribbon between your thumb and one blade of the scissors and pull toward you. It is more elegant to use the wider curling ribbon for your bouquet.

Clothespin clip

When you are ready to deliver the bouquet, hold the balloons and the ribbons as high up to the clips as possible and secure the ribbons with a clothespin. This keeps the ribbons from tangling when you go outdoors to deliver. Remove the clothespin before you hand the balloons to your customer.

Basic bouquet

11 inch latex balloons (assorted colors)
18 inch Mylar balloons
Curling ribbon (match color of balloons)
Weights
Cards

Mylar basket bouquet

1. Cut the ribbons in 6 foot lengths, leaving 1 foot to curl.
2. Inflate the latex balloons until rounded.
3. Inflate the Mylar balloons using the automatic inflator. The regulator will shut off when the balloon is inflated to the maximum.
4. Seal the Mylar balloon with the heat sealer. Test the seal on the neck of the balloon in a glass of water, if bubbles appear it is not sealed properly.
5. Tie the ribbons to the balloons and add the weight.

BASKETS

A great way to expand your balloon business is to combine with gift baskets. Attach three to five balloons to a basket and increase your sales profit.

Customers will buy the baskets for table centerpieces and also for individual gifts. Men and women both purchase baskets for gifts. Many professional people do not have time or left over energy to shop for gifts. This is where you come in as a home-based business. The business world is always looking for unique and clever new gifts.

When pricing your creation ascertain the cost of your supplies, then multiply by four.

If an order is large enough, for a fee, you can offer to deliver the baskets right to their offices. Be sure to buy your baskets wholesale.

When assembling a gift basket, do the following:

1. Originality: Create your own designs. Do not have a copy of the baskets customers can buy in a shopping mall. Don't mix food and fragrances.

2. Shape: Consider the size, shape and color of the basket. Oval is the most popular, because most baskets with handles are oval.

3. Contents: What is the theme of the basket? Select a main product and build around it. Products similar in size help balance the basket. I usually try to have something tall in the center. Achieving height in a design promotes perceived value. If you are using a tall bottle, use florist wire to tie the neck to the handle of the basket so it won't fall.

4. Use shredded paper as filler underneath the decorative straw. Sprinkle metallic grass over the straw to give a sparkling effect.

5. Customers won't buy a basket unless they like the product inside. Use quality products and charge accordingly.

6. Color/Texture: Coordinate your colors to the theme of the basket. Don't use more than three colors. Bring the colors together with a bow of all three. Choose a texture fitting to the theme. If it is for a woman, use a hatbox. If you're designing a food basket for a man you could put a bag of pretzels in a burlap bag or use a top hat upside down as a basket.

7. Shrink wrap decorative cellophane by placing a large piece over the basket and tape it on the underside. Use a high-powered hair dryer or professional heat gun to shrink the cellophane and give the basket that "store-bought look."

8. Finish the basket with a large bow. You can place it on the handle or to the side. If it is a Christmas basket, put a sprig of holly on the bow.

9. Remember to tape your business card on the bottom of the basket.

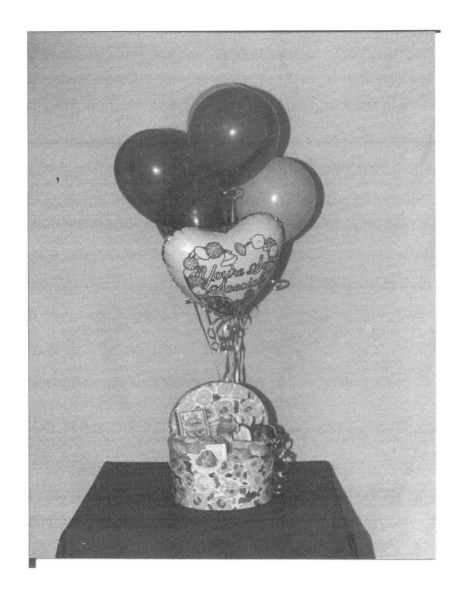

Floral Hat Box

Contents: Heart shape soap, hand lotion, shower and bath gel, bath cubes, glycerin soap, body lotion, Angel face note pad and a silk rose.

Sundae Best

Contents: Ice cream scoop, two sundae glasses, spoons, box of cookies (long and narrow in size) sundae toppings and a jar of nuts. Fill sundae glasses with color tissue paper.

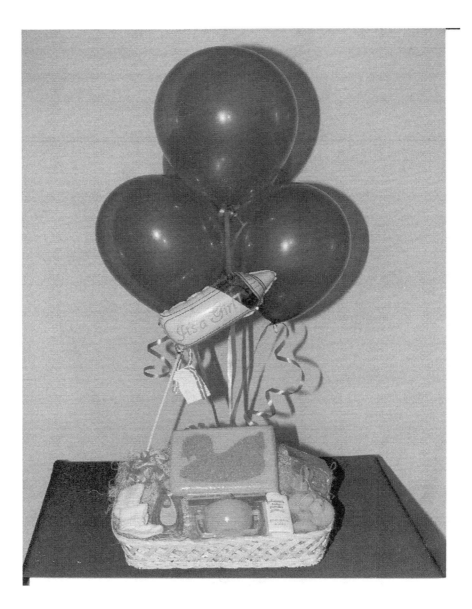

Rubber Ducky Shower Basket

Contents   Three-pack rubber ducks, duck bath sponge, duck night-light, baby shampoo, baby oil, baby powder, booties, and a cute baby book. Add a baby bottle shaped Mylar balloon.

Italian Wine Basket

Contents: Wine, pasta, French bread, olive oil, garlic, wooden spaghetti fork, wine glasses, spaghetti sauce, a cluster of fresh grapes, and two napkins,

Father's Day Special
Contents: Duck telephone, and love.

Champagne and Hearts

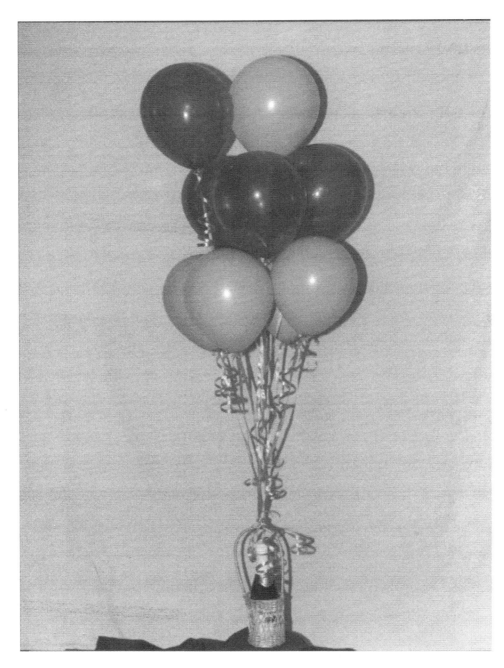

Champagne in a Basket

CHAPTER NINE

ARCHES

SINGLE ARCH:

The Single Arch is made on 50# test white string arch line. The string arch line will hold tight on the neck of the balloon with just a single loop around the base. Do not use monofilament, or the loop will loosen and release your balloon.

The single arch is a more economical design for the client but it will look sparse if only one arch is used behind the main table or across the dance floor. Four single arches from each corner of a dance floor gives a pretty umbrella design.

When measuring for the arch add 10 feet to the length for height and four feet for tying to your weights. A 25-foot length arch will use 39 feet of arch line. You will charge the customer for a 35-foot arch.

SUPPLIES:
50# test arch line
Tying discs
Weights
Foil
Ribbon
11" balloons
Helium
2 chairs

STEP 1:   Place two chairs apart (the length of the arch you are making) and tie the arch line to the chairs using the extra two feet you measured for tying.

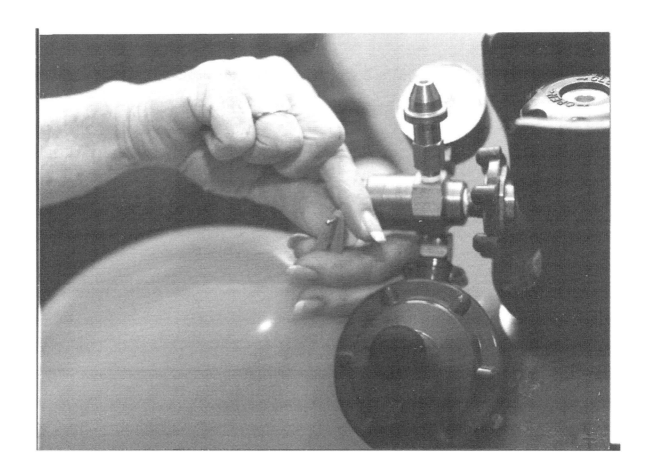

STEP 2:   Place tying discs on the disc tying post. Inflate your first balloon to the proper size using your 11" template. All balloons must be the same size to create a professional design. Stretch the neck of the balloon over the disc tying post.

66

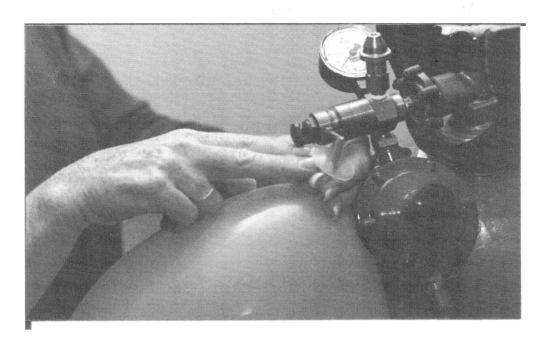

STEP 3: Slide discover the end of the post and down one-inch on the balloon neck.

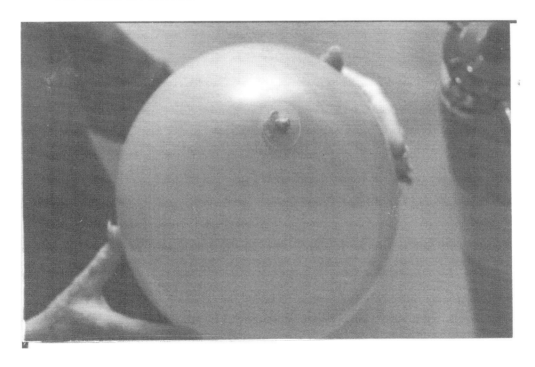

STEP 4: Place the balloon on the string by making a small loop in the
string. Slip the loop between the clip and the neck of the
balloon. Pull the loop tight. Slide the balloon to the desired
position. Each balloon should slightly touch the other.

68

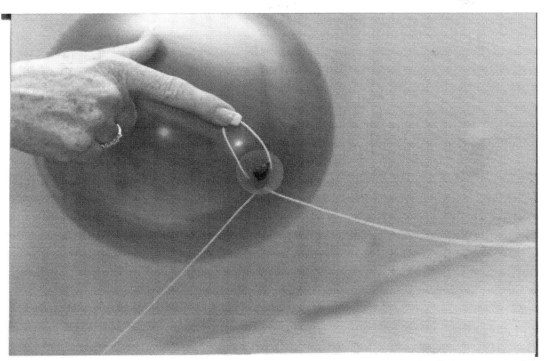

Loop the string on the neck of the balloon, pull tight and slide to position

STEP 5:
Use half of a brick wrapped in foil for your weight. Tie the weights to each end of the arch line and add a large bow for cover. You may also use 16" balloons filled with sand, heavy-duty tape if on a tile floor, or floral pins if on carpet to secure the arch. Check to see that the balloons at the base are even at both ends.

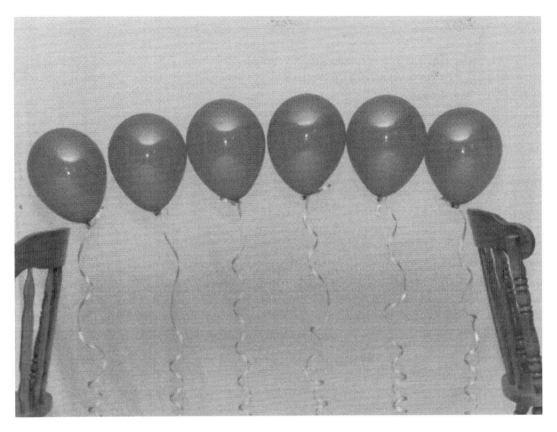

DESIGNS:

Five-foot matching color ribbons may be attached when you are clipping the balloons for a more full effect.

You may want to add a small 5" air filled balloon to the bottom of each balloon or add a small bow. Don't forget to charge more.

Alternate silver Mylar stars with gold Mylar moon shaped balloons for an outdoor evening dance.

On Valentine's Day, make the entire arch out of heart shaped balloons.

Outdoors or Indoors

More Designs

And more

THE SPIRAL QUAD ARCH

The Spiral Quad Arch will be the most profitable and most popular of all your designs. Use 50# test monofilament (fishing line) instead of the white arch line string used in the single arch. The neck of the balloon rubs on the coarseness of the string and this causes leaks. This does not happen with the smooth monofilament line.

Again, measure the arch line as you did for the single arch adding ten feet for height and two feet at each end for tying weights.

SUPPLIES:

        50# test monofilament fishing line
        weights/foil
        ribbon
        11" balloons
        helium
        2 chairs
        Christmas lights (optional)

STEP 1:   Put two chairs [the length of the arch you are making] apart and tie the arch line to the chairs.

STEP 2:   Inflate several balloons; clip with the tying disc, and immediately place them on the line every six feet. This is to prevent people from walking into your arch line.

STEP 3:   Select your color pattern for your arch and lay the balloons out in the same order. Inflate the balloon to the proper size using your 11" template. All balloons **MUST** be the same size. <u>Do not</u> clip with the tying disc. You may select one to four colors in your design. The two-color combination is the most popular design.

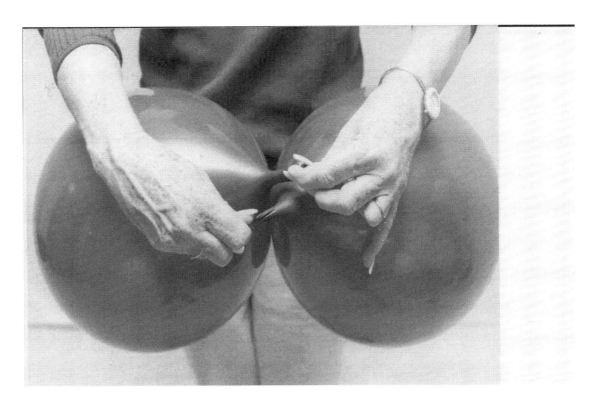

STEP 4: Tie two of the same color balloons together (for example we will use blue & white) as you would a shoelace. Next, tie two of the other color together.

Spiral quad arch two color combination.

Twist the two sets of balloons together

A quad set with two colors touching each other

STEP 5: Split the blue and white balloons
as you put them on the line.

With a blue balloon in one hand and a white balloon in the other, twist the two balloons on the line. This creates a quad in which every other balloon is an opposite color.

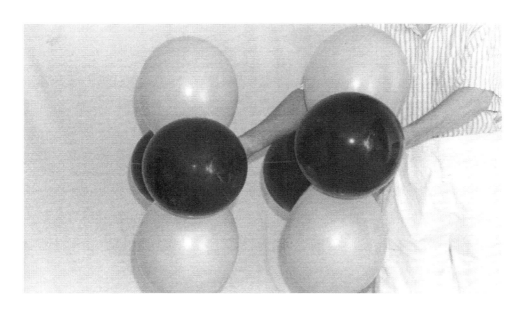

STEP 6: Slide the second quad against the grooves of the first quad. To start the spiral, the blue balloon in the second quad will be turned 1/4 turn to the right of the other blue.

1/4 turn to the right of the same color forms the spiral

Keep repeating this step until the arch is complete.

STEP 8: Tie to your weights and add a bow. You may also weave in the miniature white Christmas lights. These lights will not heat up enough to pop your balloons.

STEP 9: If any of your balloons deflate in your arch, inflate another balloon of the same color. Open a paper clip slightly, and push it through the neck of the balloon below the knot. Reach in where the deflated balloon was and attach the paper clip to the neck of the opposing balloon.

DESIGNS:
Some variations of the arch depend upon the colors you use or the spiral design. One design is to use one solid color for five sets and then five sets of another or even a third color. This will give a checker board effect.

Double spiral arch is achieved by two of the same colors side by side. Below: Completed double spiral.

Finished arches

CHAPTER TEN

OUTDOOR DECORATING

The best advice I can give you, as a beginning balloon decorator regarding outdoor decorating is, BE SELECTIVE!

Unless your event is between the months of October and February around five p.m. and the weather report is guaranteed to be cool and clear, don't accept it. If you can meet all these requirements, then you will be fine.

If you still insist on booking outside jobs, be prepared for the elements. There won't be a hint of wind until you blow up your first balloon. I have built arches inside garages, under patios, inside large empty buildings, and always encountered huge problems.

A rental supply company contracted me to build a 75-foot arch and put it in front of their storefront on a Friday afternoon for their grand opening party that evening. I asked a real estate office across the street if I could use an empty building next to them to build it inside. We squeezed the arch out the front door of the building and into the parking lot just to get it built. It took five of us to walk it across a busy street and place it in front of the building. Traffic was stopped for a block, not because we stopped them, but they were watching us. I weighted the arch with bricks and sand bags and HEAVY PRAYER.

One man driving by shouted "Where's the parade?"

We finished the job; the company was delighted; We were exhausted.

If you attempt an outside arch, be sure you use at least a 80# test monofilament line because you need a heavy line to attach to the balloons. Pack the quads of balloons in tight with each other. Do not attempt to do single arches as the wind will blow and twist them.

Balloon bouquets are difficult to keep from twisting when the wind hits them. Gather the ribbons in your hand up toward the neck of the bouquet and use a clip on the ribbons to hold them tightly until you deliver them. Remove the clip once you are inside the building. This prevents the ribbons from tangling.

I made balloon flower trees for an outdoor wedding out of a quad with two five inch balloons in between them. Then put them on a three-quarter

inch wooden dowel (use white paint) and stuck them in the ground along a driveway.

These balloon flowers were air filled. This is very attractive for an outdoor wedding reception. It lines the driveway as the guests come in. the balloons are filled with air.

88

Arches over a swimming pool for backyard parties are beautiful, but tend to sway in the wind, and need to be weighted.

For a pool reception, float the bride and groom
.

Pool decorating is very festive for an outdoor party. You can make balloon flowers with air. Tie a weight to one end of the monofilament line. Tie to the quad. This serves as a weight to the bottom of the pool. The flowers float and look great if the hostess adds some under water pool lighting.

Add a Mylar star

BALLOON DROP BAG INSTRUCTIONS

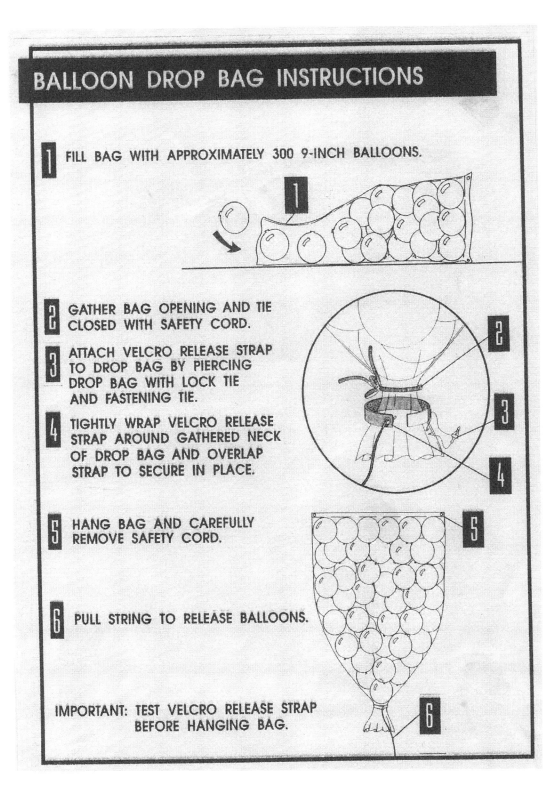

1 FILL BAG WITH APPROXIMATELY 300 9-INCH BALLOONS.

2 GATHER BAG OPENING AND TIE CLOSED WITH SAFETY CORD.

3 ATTACH VELCRO RELEASE STRAP TO DROP BAG BY PIERCING DROP BAG WITH LOCK TIE AND FASTENING TIE.

4 TIGHTLY WRAP VELCRO RELEASE STRAP AROUND GATHERED NECK OF DROP BAG AND OVERLAP STRAP TO SECURE IN PLACE.

5 HANG BAG AND CAREFULLY REMOVE SAFETY CORD.

6 PULL STRING TO RELEASE BALLOONS.

IMPORTANT: TEST VELCRO RELEASE STRAP BEFORE HANGING BAG.

CHAPTER ELEVEN

HELIUM FREE DESIGNS

There are many unique sculptures to make with free air. I worked with a boss who was dreading his fiftieth birthday so I wanted to offer my condolences. I made a four-foot wreath out of five-inch balloons. I found a "in sympathy" sign in gold used for funerals at my local florist shop and laid it from end to end on the wreath. To finish it, I added:

Preparation H	Denture cleaner
Ex-lax tablets	Geritol capsules
Eye glass cleaners	Nytol tablets

He was so surprised. So was I when he said I might not be employed here!

Balloons can be used for any age or gender. The hard-to-buy for man would enjoy dark green or blue air-filled or helium balloons attached to a gourmet basket of wine and cheese. Bottles of wine or champagne wrapped in rust or green cellophane with balloons attached are another favorite gift.

NUMBERS AND LETTERS

Great sources of business are colleges, especially the fraternities and sororities. They enjoy having their Greek letters made up in balloons for formal dances. The letters can be suspended in the lobby or on the wall in the large hotel ballrooms.

Also, many pre-school families buy a 6-foot number (2,3,4,) made of balloons to put on their front yard for their toddlers birthday parties.

To form a name with balloons:

STEP 1: Use aluminum tubing or heavy gauge wire used for chain link fence.

STEP 2: Make a chalk outline of the name.

STEP 3: Form the wire over the outline.

STEP 4: Fill clusters of three air-filled balloons, five-inch size.

STEP 5: Twist the clusters on the wire and pack tight with each cluster.

STEP 6: Attach monofilament line to the top so you can hang it if necessary.

My first experience with letters was spelling out "Julie" and the woman wanted it in hand writing, not individual letters. I was glad her name wasn't ANASTASIA!

Numbers are basically the same as the letters. They can be made out of PVC pipe, aluminum tubing or heavy gauge bendable fence wire

95

purchased at a hardware store. Or if your budget permits these are available at the balloon supply stores.

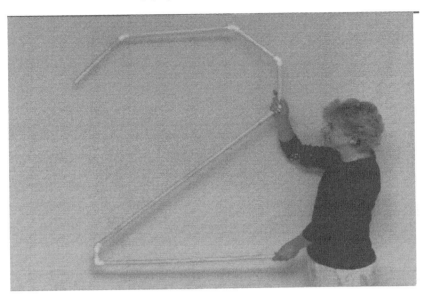

Popular numbers are the "25" and the "50" for anniversaries. This "2" is assembled out of PVC pipe.

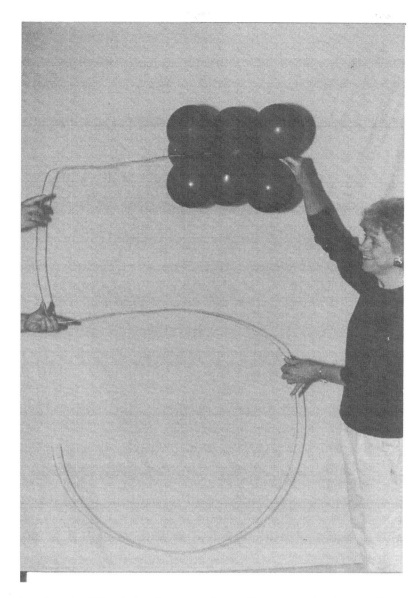

Tie three five-inch air-filled balloons together and place the cluster on the pre-formed heavy gauge fence wire.

This is a 6 foot tall "9" and "0" of gold and royal blue for a
gentleman's 90th birthday. It was a great background
for family pictures.

Three Balloon Cluster

Form the letters with the heavy gauge wire, and attach the three balloon clusters. Pictured is a "Q"

To achieve the spiral design, tie two of one color with one of a different color. Rotate the single color 1/4 turn each time.

HEART

Sketch a five-foot tall heart shape in chalk on the garage floor or driveway. Form the heart with the heavy gauge fence wire. It will take approximately 15 feet of wire. Secure the center point with masking tape. Tie the three balloon cluster sets together and twist on to the heart form. This will create a 7 foot high finished heart.

To suspend the heart from the ceiling, tie monofilament line from the left arch of the heart to the right arch. Tie a second line to the center of the first line and then to the ceiling. This will allow the heart to be adjusted left or right to a perfect perpendicular position.

Heart with netting draped from the center

Freestanding heart
Below: Freestanding PVC Heart Frame

BALLOON TREES

Balloon trees are wonderful to place in vacant spots that need color. They can be placed on the end of a stage in a large hall to give a full look to the room. The trees can stand on each side of a speaker's podium. The audience can enjoy the balloons even if the speaker is boring.

Put a balloon tree on each corner of a dance floor with flowing wide ribbon touching the floor. Attach the trees to a single arch on all four sides of the dance floor, giving a "framed-in" look.

My favorite creation is my "daisy tree". This is a popular item for weddings. With the bride's permission, set the daisy tree on the bar with a cardholder and your business cards. You will be amazed how many people will pick up your card and give you a call, especially a future bride. They have seen your work and like it. What better referral could you have?

The daisy tree is perfect to place on the guest sign-in table. I have placed them as table centerpieces at Christmas parties in hotels.

DAISY TREE

SUPPLIES:

6 inch wide basket

5" square Styrofoam

Six 5" latex balloons

Four 11" latex heart balloons

Color tissue paper

Ribbon 2" wide for bow

5/16" diameter 24" long wooden dowel

Daisy Tree

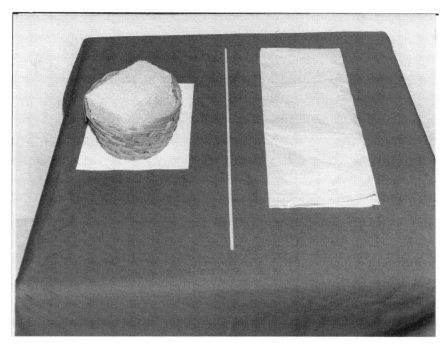

Basket, Styrofoam, Dowel, & Tissue paper

Cut a piece of 5" Styrofoam square and wrap in colorful tissue paper, place it inside the basket snug. Place the dowel into the center of the Styrofoam. Inflate four 5" balloons, twist two together and wrap the four balloons around the dowel.

Air-fill four heart balloons. Twist two together and wrap around at the top of the dowel. Inflate two 5" balloons and insert them between the top four balloons forming the bud. You can wrap narrow ribbon around the dowel or leave it solid. Make a bow with 2" ribbon. Attach it to the front of the basket.

Twisting the hearts and center

Completed Daisy Tree

107

BASIC PVC STAND

The basic PVC (plastic water sprinkler pipe) stand will be used for most freestanding forms. You will need a 10-foot length of 1/2" PVC pipe for each stand. This pipe cost about $3 at your local discount hardware stores.

From this pipe cut the following:

Other PVC supplies:

6 pieces of 6 inch lengths,
2 pieces of 13 inch lengths,
2 pieces of 2 ft 3 inch lengths

4 each 90 degree elbows
3 each tee's
1 each coupling
1 each PVC glue
1 bag of sand
1 funnel

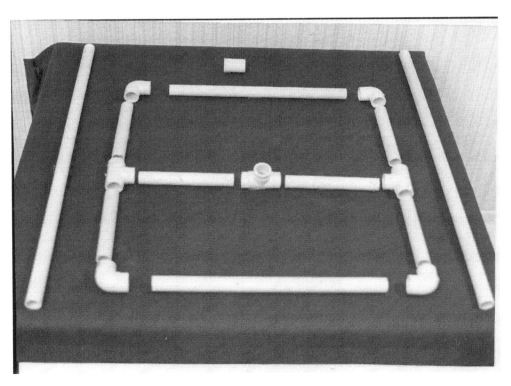

Assemble and glue the stand as shown on page 128. It will fit easier for transportation if you do not glue the two upright center poles until you are at the job sight. The basic PVC stand will hold seven sets of quads on top of each other and will give you a six-foot standing sculpture. If you wish your sculpture to be 7, 8, 9, or 10 feet high, cut the center pole to the desired length. Use a funnel and sand to fill the base of the basic stand to give stability.

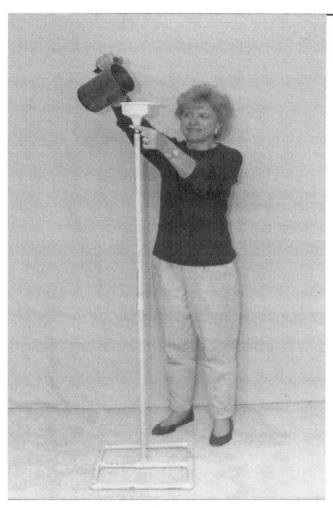

FLOWER TREE
Fill the base of the stand with sand

109

The flower tree is another of my own designs. Balloon trees have been done before, but I created this particular one.

SUPPLIES:

Basic PVC base with a six-foot center pole.
8 each heart shape latex balloons
2 each 9" latex balloons
8 each 11" latex balloons
2" wide ribbon
  sand for the base

1. Pour sand down into the base to weight the stand. Shake it around to even the weight.

2. Wrap the ribbon around the pole like a barber pole.

3. Air-fill four latex 11" heart shape balloons and twist making a quad. Set aside and make a second quad. Air- fill two latex 9" balloons and tie together. Hold the two quads together and insert the 9" balloons in between securing them together.

4. Place the double quad around the top of the pole by wrapping one balloon over another.

5. Air-fill the 8 latex 11" balloons and make two quads and twist them around the base of the pole just above the base.

6. Make a large bow and tie it on the pole anywhere you choose.

Wrap the ribbon like a barber pole

Two quads 11" latex hearts

Insert the 9" latex balloons between quads

Side view of quads

Front view of quads

114

Add the 11" round latex balloons to the base

CHAPTER TWELVE

BALLOON FRIENDS

What a wonderful world it would be if we could create the "perfect friend." I will show you how you can do just that.

A large hotel chain called me and asked if I could make a balloon butler to greet guests for their grand opening. I made the sculpture using the basic PVC stand. The jacket was made of black eleven-inch balloons and the pants were garnet wine. With a top hat and a white towel provided by the hotel, our butler was the hit of the evening.

A high school requested a boy and girl balloon person to sit in an old car for a dance. Using yellow yarn for the girl's hair and black yarn for the boy's sideburns, we filled the order. This was an quick and easy job. I built them from the waist up and put them in the front seat. It reminded me of some of my past boyfriends who were only "half" there!

BASIC RECIPE FOR A BALLOON FRIEND

SUPPLIES:

Basic PVC stand, measure center pole 5 ft.
Eight sets of 11" air-filled quads (4 balloons tied)
One quad of 5" air-filled balloons for the neck.
Air-filled 16" balloon (optional color) for the head.
Add accessories

STEP 1:   Assemble the basic PVC stand and pour in sand for weight and stability. Note: For the groom paint the bottom half of the stand black.

STEP 2:   Stack eight quad sets of balloons on the PVC pole; twist one balloon over the other to secure the quad. Place all eight sets on top of each other. Place one set in the groove of the other.

STEP 3:   Inflate the 16" balloon head to the proper size. Attach 2 feet of balloon string to the neck. Pull the string down tight through the second quad from the top. Wrap several times between two alternating balloons.

STEP 4:   Air-fill four 5" balloons and place on the pole under the 16" balloon to support the head.

STEP 5:   Add accessories.

These directions are for any balloon friend. Just add a scarf and hat for a snowman. Add wings for an angel, a towel for a butler, or a party hat and a big bow tie to make a clown. If you are creating a bride and groom, you can add a top hat and veil. Top hats can be purchased at a party shop or craft store for approximately $3.99. After New Year's Eve, buy the top hats at 1/2 price.

GROOM

SUPPLIES:

Basic PVC stand - 4 foot 6 inch

4 quads of air-filled black latex 11" balloons (pants)

3 quads of air-filled white latex 11" balloons (shirt)

1 quad of air-filled white latex 5" balloons (collar)

1 16" white air-filled latex balloon (head)

1 black top hat

1 bow tie & mustache (see patterns on pp. 147 & 149)

Two-sided tape and bottle of rubber cement

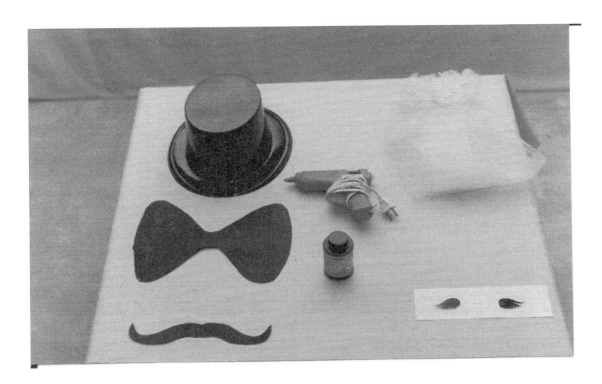

Supplies for Bride & Groom

ASSEMBLING THE GROOM

STEP 1:   Place four quads of black balloons on the pole.

STEP 2:   Place three quads of white balloons on top to make the shirt.

STEP 3:   Tie the neck of the 16" white balloon with arch string. Place on top of the seven quad sets and wrap the excess string around one of the quads.

STEP 4:   To make the collar, place 1 quad of 5" white balloons under the neck of the 16" head to support it.

STEP 5: Attach two pieces of two-sided tape on the underside of the top hat. Place it on top of the 16" white balloon.

STEP 6: Place rubber cement on the mustache and position it on the face.

STEP 7: Center the bow tie and attach it with rubber cement.

Groom's pants

121

Head & collar

Groom fully dressed

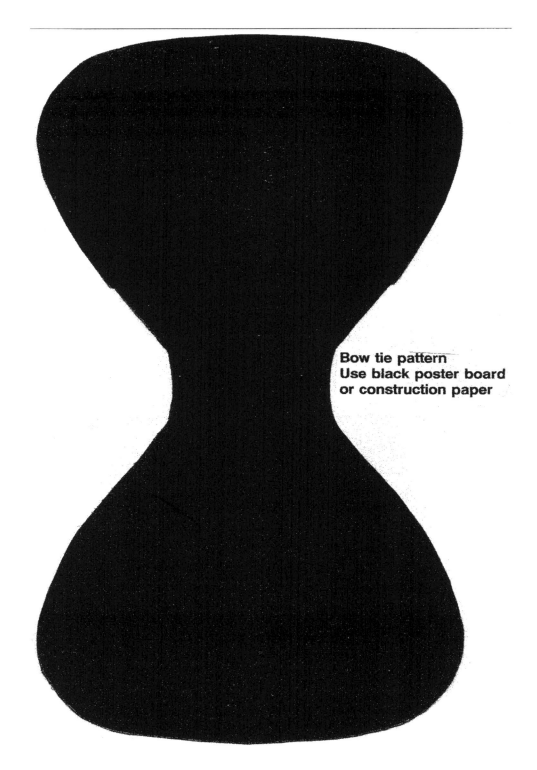

Bow tie pattern
Use black poster board
or construction paper

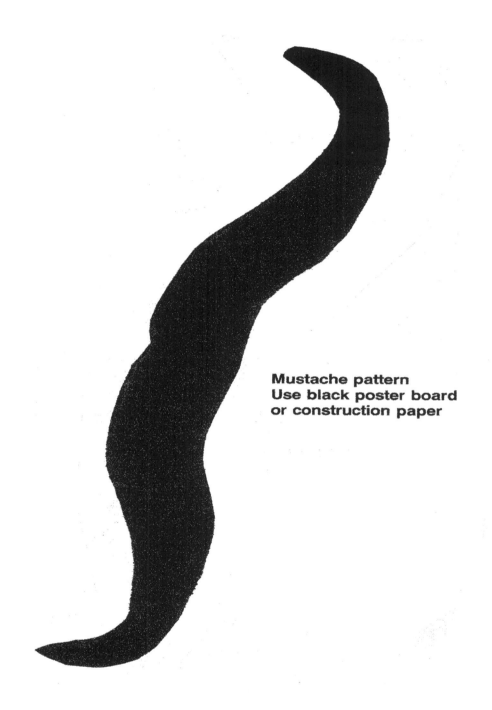

**Mustache pattern
Use black poster board
or construction paper**

BRIDE

SUPPLIES:

    Basic PVC stand - 4 foot 6 inch pole
7 quads of 11" white air-filled balloons (bridal dress)
1 quad of 5" white air-filled balloons (necklace)
1 16" white latex air-filled balloon (head)
1 square yard of white net
1 small cluster of white silk flowers
1 set of false eyelashes
1 bottle of rubber cement.

ASSEMBLING THE BRIDE

STEP 1:   Place seven quads of white balloons on the pole.

STEP 2:   Tie the neck of the 16" white balloon with arch string. Place on top of the seven quad sets and wrap the excess string around one of the quads.

STEP 3:   To make the pearls, place 1 quad of 5" white balloons under the neck of the 16" head to support it.

STEP 4:   Trim the eyelashes to the size needed. Use rubber cement and place them on the face.

STEP 5:   Hot glue a small cluster of flowers in the middle of the square yard of netting.

STEP 6:   Place the veil over the top of the 16" white balloon head.

Stacking the quads on the center pole.

Assembling the head and necklace

The bride's pearls.

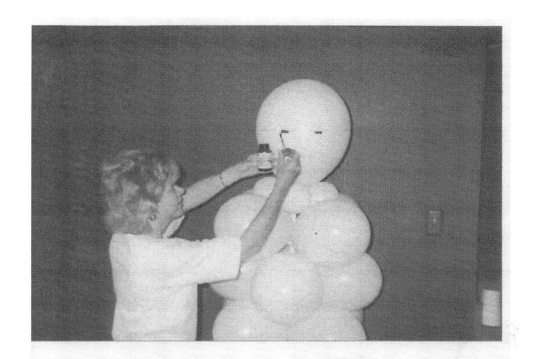

Eyelashes & veil

The Beautiful Bride

132

CLOWN

SUPPLIES:

Basic PVC stand - 5 foot pole

8 quads of 11" jewel-tone air-filled balloons

1 quad of 5" balloons (neck)

11 5" red balloons (eyes, ears, nose,& mouth)

44 5" yellow balloons (arms)

1 16" white latex air-filled balloon (head)

2 16" white latex air-filled balloons (feet)

1 clown hat (purchase at party shop)

1 bow tie (in red or yellow)

ASSEMBLING THE CLOWN

This clown could sell for $150.00. It is made with
air balloons and will last for several days.

CHAPTER THIRTEEN

WEDDINGS

Gone are the days of crepe paper streamers across the ceiling. Balloons are the decorations of the times.

Show the client how you can transform a dull banquet room into an elegant masterpiece. Balloons brighten up dark walls and poor lighting, and of course, create a festive atmosphere.

Let's cover planning and decorating for a wedding. Make an appointment with the bride and groom. Ask them who is paying for the balloon decorations. If it is someone other than the bride or groom, make sure that person comes with them to the appointment. You may find yourself spending time with a couple that selects $1,000 worth of decorations only to call back the next day to say, We decided that was too much to spend."

Ask if the appointment is convenient for all the involved parties. After the meeting ask for a deposit of half the cost, so you will have a commitment for the date. Purchase a "NO REFUND" hand stamp. Stamp the bottom of the invoice and ask the clients to sign it.

Ask the bride to bring a sample of the bridesmaids dress material if she is creating her balloon theme with their colors. Inflate the balloons so she will see the colors you will use for her wedding reception. No surprises on the "big day!"

Sometimes the bride will picture a color more vivid than what is possible to purchase in balloons. Many times they depend on your expertise to help them select colors.

SPECIFIC DECORATING AREAS

CEILING BALLOONS: When the bride orders ceiling balloons over the dance floor, ask three questions: How high is the ceiling? How large is the dance floor? Are there any exposed air conditioning ducts that will blow the balloons to one corner and destroy the design? A catering manager will have this information.

If the ceiling is over eighteen-feet tall, the balloons are too high. All you will see is the ribbon hanging down. Arrange the ceiling balloons so that they are spread out over the dance area. The minimum ceiling balloons you should use is one hundred fifty balloons. If it is a large area to cover, use two hundred to two hundred fifty.

Measure the ribbons so they are at least seven feet above the floor. Not many guests are over 7 ft. tall so the ribbons won't be hanging in their faces.

GUEST TABLES: Attach the balloons and curling ribbon to the centerpieces. Measure the ribbon in three, four, and five-foot lengths. Match the color of the ribbon to the color of the balloon. This gives a professional look. The length of the ribbons will float the balloons high enough for guests to talk across the table. It saves time to pre-cut your ribbons at home.

HEAD TABLE: Several tables are put together on a raised platform and draped. The bride, groom, and the attendants are seated here. A spiral quad arch looks beautiful behind the head table. Be sure there is ample room for the wedding party to walk between the table and the arch.

A large balloon heart suspended from the ceiling can be centered behind the bridal table.

ENTRANCE: The area for the arriving guests to register. The balloon bride and groom are often placed on the inside of the door to greet the guests. Use a "daisy tree" on the sign in table.

MUSIC AREA: It is festive to build a single arch over the DJ, and add bouquets on each speaker. The lights reflect on the balloons. If a band will be performing on the stage, you would have several choices. A spiral quad arch, balloon trees, or several single arches giving a tunnel effect.

DANCE FLOOR: I designed a gift package to put around the edge of the dance floor. One company bought five pound boxes of candy to place inside. After dinner, they raffled off the gift boxes. These can be used for many different occasions by changing the wrapping.

SUPPLIES: (one gift package)
    12x18 box with a removable lid
    4 9" latex helium filled balloons
    1 40" latex helium filled balloon of desired color.
    15 feet of sheer tulle (net)
    Brick wrapped in foil
    10 yards of 2 inch wide ribbon

ASSEMBLING THE GIFT PACKAGE

STEP 1:   Cover the box and the lid with white wrapping paper if it is for a wedding. Red wrapping is used for Christmas dances.

STEP 2:   Wrap the tulle around the brick, place it inside the box.

STEP 3:   Make a slit in the top of the box approximately 5" long and feed the tulle through the slit to the outside, until you have the desired height.

STEP 4:   Attach the helium inflated 40" balloon by tying the tulle to the neck of the balloon.

141

STEP 5:   Make a quad of the 4 helium inflated 9" balloons
           and place them at the neck of the 40" balloon.

Completed gift package design

CHAPTER FOURTEEN

HOLIDAY DECORATING

Decorating with balloons for the holidays can be very profitable. Contact the hotels within a fifty-mile radius. Christmas decorating is well worth the traveling. Deck the Halls! Fill the ballrooms with air balloon Christmas trees, candy canes and Santa Claus.

You need to start contacting large companies and hotels in October. Build a Christmas balloon tree at home and take an 8x10 photo. Have several prints made. Put it in an inexpensive frame and leave one with the catering managers. Be sure you leave your cards with it. Ask them to set it up near their desk where they interview their clients. You will be amazed how many calls you will receive for holiday decorating.

Send your cards to the high schools to remind them you are available to decorate for their Christmas Ball or Winter Formal. Elementary schools usually have a Christmas program before closing for their vacation. Balloon angels flying above a Christmas pageant will make a performance special.

Christmas centerpieces can be designed with filling a red wooden sleigh with candy and three red and green helium filled balloons.

Poinsettia plants and balloons are a popular take-home centerpiece.

CHRISTMAS TREE:

SUPPLIES:

Basic PVC stand - 5-foot pole.
2 quads of air-filled emerald green 16" balloons
3 quads of air-filled emerald green 11" balloons
1 quad of air-filled emerald green 9" balloons
1 quad of air-filled emerald green 7" balloons
2 quads of air-filled emerald green 5" balloons
15 air-filled ruby red 5" balloons
1 treetop angel with a miniature light in the top
2 strands of miniature lights

ASSEMBLING THE CHRISTMAS TREE

STEP 1:   Attach two quads of 16" balloons on the PVC pole.

STEP 2:   Put three quads of 11" balloons followed by one quad of 9" and one quad of 7" balloons.

STEP 3:   Place the quads of 5" balloons on top of each other, and rubber cement together. Position this group on top of the tree.

STEP 4:   A lighted angel on top of the balloons completes the tree.

STEP 5:   Wrap the tree with the miniature lights. Stand the tree near an electrical outlet to plug in the lights and the angel.

146

STEP 6: Inflate the fifteen ruby red 5" balloons. Use rubber cement to insert them all over the tree to look like ornaments.

5" tree top

Adding angel top and miniature lights

CHRISTMAS WREATH

SUPPLIES:

10-foot piece heavy gauge fence wire

26 tri-sets of air-filled 5" emerald green balloons

4 tri-single air-filled 5" ruby red balloons

1 large red bow with long streamers

Babies breath or silk holly (optional)

ASSEMBLING THE CHRISTMAS WREATH

STEP 1:   Bend the wire into a ring and secure the ends with green florist tape.

STEP 2:   Wrap five-inch balloons in clusters of three and place them on the wire. Keep repeating and slide each into the groove of the other securely.

STEP 3:   Place the five inch ruby red balloons in between the clusters to look like berries or ornaments. Hold them in place with rubber cement.

STEP 4   Hang the wreath with monofilament line.

STEP 5:   Place a large red bow in the center top of the wreath. Place bunches of babies breath or silk holly leaves in with the five inch red balloons. Add Christmas lights.

ANGEL

SUPPLIES:

Basic PVC stand - 5-foot pole

8 quads of air-filled white 11" latex balloons

1 quad of air-filled white 5" latex balloons

1 16" white air-filled latex balloon

1 pair of angel wings (purchase at craft store)

1 skein of yellow yarn

1 set of false eyelashes

Bottle of rubber cement

STEP 1:   Place eight quads on the center pole.

STEP 2:   Tie the 16" head to the center pole and wrap excess string around the other balloons.

STEP 4:   Attach the angel wings by pulling the elastic straps around the balloons in the back of the angel.

STEP 5:   Secure the skein of yarn to the head with rubber cement. Cut and arrange the strands as a hairpiece.

STEP 6:   Rubber cement the eyelashes onto the face.

Christmas Angel

SNOW MAN

SUPPLIES:

Basic PVC stand - 5-foot pole
8 quads of 11" white latex air-filled balloons

1 quad of 5" white latex air-filled balloons

1 16" white air-filled balloon

1 ruby red 5" (nose)

2 black 5" balloons (eyes)

Winter plaid neck scarf

Black derby hat

Large red bow with four-foot length ties

STEP 1: Place eight quads on the center pole.

STEP 2: Tie the 16" head to the center pole. Wrap excess string around the other balloons.

STEP 3: Do not fully inflate the 5" balloons. Tie and cut off the excess below the knot so it will glue flush to the face. Rubber cement the eyes and nose in place.

STEP 4:   Put double-stick tape on the inside brim of the hat and place on top of the 16" balloon. Arrange the neck scarf.

Christmas Snow Man

154

CANDY CANE

SUPPLIES:
Basic PVC stand - 5 foot Pole

5 each 12" PVC pipe

4 each 45-degree elbows

1 decorative brick for weight (see page 56)

25 quad sets 9" red & white air-filled balloons

Assembling the candy cane

STEP 1:   Place the brick over the center pole and set the PVC stand inside a Christmas wrapped box.

STEP 2:   Place the quad sets of red and white balloons on the center pole in a swirl design.

156

CHAPTER FIFTEEN

THE END AND YOUR BEGINNING

Now that you have read this handbook and studied the pictures and directions, you are on your way! Get started! It has been said, "One person can make a difference." It is true. You can make a difference in your life, and in the lives of others with your talents and new business. There is always room for new ideas in the balloon decorating world. Make yourself known and enjoy the profits from using your ideas.

I have tried to keep the steps as simple and easy as possible. But as with anything new, it takes practice and patience. I told you in previous chapters how I decorated for a friend's wedding when I was just starting. Offer to design a balloon sculpture for an event coming up with your family or friends. By doing one for free it shows them how well you can decorate.

Select several people who you can depend on, and train them using the manual to demonstrate techniques. Take them with you to the first events you book. When you can double-book jobs, you will be able to send your crew to one place and you can decorate at another. If you book five weddings on a Saturday, you can conceivably earn $1500. That is a low estimate of $300 per wedding.

Prepare early for the holidays! Start shopping in the summer months for holiday centerpieces. Stock up on green and ruby red balloons early in November. Buy miniature lights the day after Christmas when all major stores are selling them at reduced prices.

Set a goal for yourself! Spend one day a week putting out your cards. Cover a new area each week.

I am excited for you in just writing this book. I remember how I was always amazed each time the telephone rang the first months of my new business. People needed my help and expertise. And I was getting paid TOO.

There is a famous author, Marshall McLuhan, who wrote "Beware. The present has turned a corner when you were not looking, and you have been dangerously left behind."

You can do it! Just get started. Good luck and have fun

"The Bride's Ride"

About the Author

With only a bag of balloons, a helium tank, and lot of determination, Ruth Younger started a home-based balloon enterprise that has flourished into a highly successful balloon decorating business. She has shared her creativity and resourcefulness with hundreds of students in her popular small business seminars to help students start their own profitable business. In addition, she is a teacher and conducts classes in Senior Theater and Writing Memoirs.

Visit the author's website at:
www.balloonsmanual.com

Contact the author by email at:
info@balloonmanual.com